THE DIDACHE : TEACHING OF THE TWELVE APOSTLES

AND THE EPISTLE OF BARNABAS

Translated by
PHILIP SCHAFF

CONTENTS

INTRODUCTORY NOTICE

1. The discovery of the codex, and its contents.   3
2. Publication of the discovered works: the effect.   5
3. Contents of teaching, and relation to other works.   7
4. Authenticity.   10
5. Time and place of composition.   14

THE DIDACHE : TEACHING OF
THE TWELVE APOSTLES

1. The Two Ways; The First Commandment.   21
2. The Second Commandment: Gross Sin Forbidden.   23
3. Other Sins Forbidden.   25
4. Various Precepts.   27
5. The Way of Death.   30
6. Against False Teachers, and Food Offered to Idols.   32
7. Concerning Baptism.   33
8. Concerning Fasting and Prayer (the Lord's Prayer).   34
9. The Thanksgiving (Eucharist).   35
10. Prayer After Communion.   37
11. Concerning Teachers, Apostles, and Prophets.   39
12. Reception of Christians.   41
13. Support of Prophets.   42
14. Christian Assembly on the Lord's Day.   43
15. Bishops and Deacons; Christian Reproof.   44
16. Watchfulness; The Coming of the Lord.   45

THE EPISTLE OF BARNABAS

Introductory Note to the Epistle of Barnabas	49
1. After the salutation, the writer declares that he would communicate to his brethren something of that which he had himself received.	55
2. The Jewish sacrifices are now abolished.	57
3. The fasts of the Jews are not true fasts, nor acceptable to God.	59
4. Antichrist is at hand: let us therefore avoid Jewish errors.	61
5. The new covenant, founded on the sufferings of Christ, tends to our salvation, but to the Jews' destruction.	64
6. The sufferings of Christ, and the new covenant, were announced by the prophets.	67
7. Fasting, and the goat sent away, were types of Christ.	71
8. The red heifer a type of Christ.	74
9. The spiritual meaning of circumcision.	76
10. Spiritual significance of the precepts of Moses respecting different kinds of food.	78
11. Baptism and the cross prefigured in the Old Testament.	81
12. The cross of Christ frequently announced in the Old Testament.	84
13. Christians, and not Jews, the heirs of the covenant.	87
14. The Lord hath given us the testament which Moses received and broke.	89
15. The false and the true Sabbath.	91
16. The spiritual temple of God.	93
17. Conclusion of the first part of the epistle.	96
18. Second part of the epistle. The two ways.	97
19. The way of light.	98
20. The way of darkness.	101
21. Conclusion.	103

INTRODUCTORY NOTICE

BY MATTHEW BROWN RIDDLE

1
THE DISCOVERY OF THE CODEX, AND ITS CONTENTS.

In 1873 Philotheos Bryennios, then Head Master of the higher Greek school at Constantinople, but now Metropolitan of Nicomedia, discovered a remarkable collection of manuscripts in the library of the Jerusalem Monastery of the Most Holy Sepulchre at Constantinople. This collection is bound in one volume, and written by the same hand. It is signed "Leon, notary and sinner," and bears the Greek date of 6564 = a.d. 1056. There is no reason to doubt the age of the manuscripts. The documents have been examined by Professor Albert L. Long of Robert College, Constantinople;[1] and some of the pages, reproduced by photography, were published by the Johns Hopkins University, Baltimore, April, 1885. The jealousy of its guardians does not imply any lack of confidence in the age and value of the Codex. The contents of the 120 folios (240 pp.) are as follows:—

I. Synopsis of the Old and New Testaments, by St. Chrysostom (fol. 1–32).

II. The Epistle of Barnabas (fol. 33–51b).

III. The two Epistles of Clement to the Corinthians (fol. 51b-76a).

IV. The Teaching of the Twelve Apostles (fol. 76a-80).

V. The Epistle of Mary of Cassoboli to Ignatius (fol. 81–82a).

VI. Twelve Epistles of Ignatius (fol. 82a-120a).

The last part of fol. 120a contains the signature and date; then follows an account of the genealogy of Joseph, continued on the other page of the leaf.

Schaff (p. 6) gives a facsimile of fol. 120a.

Of these, I. supplies some unpublished portions, and furnishes matter for textual criticism. II. gives the second Greek copy of Barnabas, also furnishing new readings. III. is very valuable; the text of both Epistles is now complete. Two-fifths of that of the second was previously unknown. The value for purposes of textual criticism is also great. IV. is the *Teaching*, the value of which is discussed below. V. and VI. both belong to the Ignatian literature, and furnish new readings, which have already appeared in the editions of Funk (*Opera Patr. Apost.*, ii., Tübingen, 1881) and Lightfoot (*Epistles of St. Ignatius*, London and Cambridge, 1885).

---

1. See New-York *Independent*, July 31, 1884.

2

PUBLICATION OF THE DISCOVERED WORKS: THE EFFECT.

In 1875 Bryennios, who had been chosen Metropolitan of Serræ during his absence at the Old Catholic conference in Bonn, published at Constantinople the two Epistles of Clement, with prolegomena and notes; giving the text found in the Jerusalem Codex, as he termed it. All patristic scholars welcomed his work, which bore every mark of care and learning; showing the results of his contact, as a student, with German methods. Bishop Lightfoot and many others at once made use of this new material. The remaining contents of the Codex were named in the volume of Bryennios, and some interest awakened by the mention of the *Teaching*. The learned Metropolitan furnished new readings from other parts of the Codex to German scholars. At the close of 1883 he published in Constantinople the text of the *Teaching*, with prolegomena and notes. A copy of the volume was received in Germany in January, 1884; was translated into

German, and published Feb. 3, 1884; translated from German into English, and published in America, Feb. 28, 1884; Archdeacon Farrar published (*Contemporary Review*) a version from the Greek in May, 1884. Before the close of the year the literature on the subject, exclusive of newspaper articles, covered fifty titles (given by Schaff) in Western Europe and America.

3
CONTENTS OF TEACHING, AND RELATION TO OTHER WORKS.

In the Babel of conflicting opinions, it is best to notice first the obvious internal phenomena. The first part of the *Teaching* (now distinguished as chaps. i.-vi.) sets forth the duty of the Christian; in chaps. vii.-x., xiv., we find a directory for worship; chaps. xi.-xiii., xv., give advice respecting church officers, extraordinary and local, and the reception of Christians; the closing chapter (xvi.) enjoins watchfulness in view of the coming of Christ, which is then described.

The amount of matter is not so great as that of the Sermon on the Mount.

The peculiarities of language are marked, but can only be indicated here in footnotes. They point to a period of transition from New-Testament usage to that of ecclesiastical Greek. The citations from the Scriptures resemble those of the Apostolic Fathers. The Gospel of Matthew is most frequently used, especially chaps. v.-vii. and xxiv.; but some of the passages fairly imply a knowledge of the Gospel of Luke. There are some remarkable correspondences with expressions and thoughts found in the Gospel of John, while there is good reason for inferring the writer's acquaintance with all the groups of Pauline Epistles. His allusions to the other New-Testament books are less marked. There is nothing to prove that he did not know all of our canonical books. If an early date is accepted, the tone of the whole opposes the tendency-theory of the Tübingen school.

The most striking internal phenomena are, however, the correspondences of this document with early Christian writings, from a.d. 125 to the fourth century. With the so-called *Epistle to* Barnabas, chaps. xviii.-xx., the resemblances are so marked as to demand a critical theory which can account for them. A few passages in the *Shepherd of Hermas* show some resemblance; but only two sentences, in Commandment Second, are verbally the same. There is a still greater agreement with the so-called *Apostolical Church Order*, of Egyptian origin, probably as old as the third century. It is now known in the Coptic (Memphitic), and also in Arabic and Greek.[1] The first thirteen canons correspond quite closely, both in order and words, with chaps. i.-iv. of the *Teaching*.

Most noteworthy, however, is the parallel with the *Apostolic Constitutions*, vii. 1–32, which contain more than half the *Teaching*, in precisely the same order, with very close verbal resemblances. The parts omitted are in most cases such as had lost their pertinence in the fourth century, while they seem appropriate to a much earlier period. These phenomena have called forth voluminous discussions, and are the most important facts in determining the authenticity and age of the *Teaching*.

---

1. The *Church Order* is to be distinguished from the Ethiopic collection of Apostolic canons; see Introductory Notice to *Apostolic Constitutions*.

4
AUTHENTICITY.

By this is meant, in this case, the substantial identity of the recently discovered document with the work known and referred to by early Christian writers under the same (or a similar) title. Of apostolic origin no one should presume to speak, since the text of the document makes no such claim, and internal evidence is obviously against such a suggestion. On the other hand, there is no reason for doubting the age of the Codex, or the accuracy of the edition published by Bryennios.

Eusebius (d. 340) of Cæsarea, in the famous passage of his history (iii. 25) which treats of the canonical books of the New Testament, names among the "spurious" works (νόθοι) "the so-called *Teachings of the Apostles*" (τῶν ἀποστόλων αἱ λεγόμεναι διδαχαί). The plural form does not forbid a reference to the work under discussion, since Athanasius (d. 373) has a notice clearly pointing to the same writing, in which he uses the singular (*Festal Epistle*, 39). Rufinus (d. 410) speaks of a brief work called *The Two Ways*, or *The Judgment of Peter*; and this fact, in view of the contents of the *Teaching*, furnishes one of the most important data for the critical discussion. The last notice of the *Teaching* was made by Nicephorus (d. 828) more than two hundred years before Leon made this copy. Clement of Alexandria (d. circa 216) and Irenæus (*mart.* 202) use expressions that may indicate an acquaintance with this writing. The more extended correspondences with Barnabas and later disciplinary works are noticed above (sec. 3). The existence of an old Latin translation of the *Teaching*, of the tenth century, a fragment of which has been preserved, furnishes general evidence to the authenticity of the Greek copy, but by its variations suggests the presence of many textual corruptions. Its closer correspondence with Barnabas has led to the theory that the translator used both documents. Others suppose that its form points to a document which was the common source of the Greek form of the *Teaching* and of Barnabas.

The various theories based on the above facts cannot even be stated. The following positions seem, on the whole, most tenable:—

1. The Greek Codex presents substantially the writing referred to by Eusebius and Athanasius.

2. Owing to an absence of other copies, we cannot determine the purity of the text; but there is every probability of many minor corruptions.

3. This probability calls for care that we do not infer too

much from verbal resemblances.

4. The resemblances to book vii., *Apostolic Constitutions*, are, however, of such a character as establish, not only a literary connection between the two works, but also the priority of the *Teaching*

5. In the case of Barnabas, the resemblances can be accounted for (a) by accepting the priority of the *Teaching*, or (b) by assuming a common (earlier and unknown) source, or (c) by accepting the priority of Barnabas, and assuming such corruptions in the Greek copy of the *Teaching* as will account for the supposed marks of its priority. Despite the general adoption of (a), there remains a strong probability that (b) is the correct solution of the problem.

6. The Duæ Viæ, spoken of by Rufinus, may be the common source. We have no positive evidence, but the "two ways" form so prominent a topic in most of these documents which indicate literary relationship, as to encourage this theory. If there was a common source, it probably contained only matter similar to chaps. i.-v., which was variously used by the subsequent compilers. Here a number of theories have been suggested.[1] None of them, however, necessarily call for a very late date of the *Teaching*, or compel us to deny that Eusebius and Athanasius referred to substantially the same work as that now existing in the Codex at Constantinople. Many resemblances have been noticed in other works. Probably in the course of a few years all the data will have been collected,

and a well-defined result based upon them. But, even in this period of discussion, there is remarkable agreement among critics in regard to the main question of authenticity.

---

1. Compare the detailed discussions of Harnack, Holtzmann, Warfield, and most recently McGiffert, *Andover Review*, vol. v. pp. 430–442.

5
TIME AND PLACE OF COMPOSITION.

Granting the general authenticity of the Greek work, the time of composition must be at least as early as the first half of the second century. If the *Teaching* is older than Barnabas, then it cannot be later than a.d. 120. If both are from a common source, the interval of time was probably not very great. The document itself bears many marks of an early date:—

(1) Its simplicity, almost amounting to childishness, not only discountenances all idea of forgery, but points to the sub-apostolic age, during which Christianity manifested this characteristic. The fact is an important one in the discussion of the canon of the New Testament.

(2) The undeveloped Christian thought, as well as the indications of undeveloped heresy, confirms this position. Christianity was at first a life, for which the Apostles furnished a

basis of revealed thought. But the Christians of the sub-apostolic age had not consciously assimilated the thought to any large extent, while their ethical striving was stimulated by the gross sins surrounding them.

(3) The Church polity indicated in the *Teaching* is less developed than that of the genuine Ignatian Epistles, and shows the existence of extraordinary travelling teachers ("Apostles" and "Prophets," chap. xi.). This points to a date not later than the first half of the second century, probably as early as the first quarter.[1]

Most of these phenomena would, however, consist with a date as late as that of the Ignatian Epistles on the theory that the *Teaching* was written for a community of Christians in some obscure locality. But this theory must admit that there existed for a long time great variety of Church polity and worship.[2] Of this there is, indeed, considerable evidence. The undeveloped form of the doctrinal elements of the work constitutes the most serious objection to the theory of a late origin. On the other hand, it seems on many accounts improbable that the work, in its present form, was written earlier than the beginning of the second century: (1) Such a document would not be penned during the lifetime of any of the Apostles. (2) There is no allusion in chap. xvi. to the destruction of Jerusalem. If the author was a Jewish Christian, as seems most probable, such silence implies an interval of at least one generation. (3) The position of the document in the Codex is after the Clementine Epistles, and before the Ignatian. This probably marks the chronological position. (4) The extreme simplicity scarcely consists with the view that the author was nearly contemporary with the Apostles.

Bryennios and Harnack assign, as the date, between 120 and 160; Hilgenfeld, 160 and 190; English and American scholars vary between a.d. 80 and 120. Until the priority to Barnabas is more positively established, the two may be regarded as of the same age, about 120, although a date slightly later is not impossible. All attempts to discover the author are, with our present lack of data, necessarily futile. Even the region in and for which it was composed cannot be determined. Jewish-Christian tendencies are not sufficiently indicated to warrant the assumption of a polemical aim.[3] The document has been assigned to Alexandria, to Antioch, to Jerusalem; indeed, many other places have been named. In favour of the Syrian origin is the literary connection with the *Apostolic Constitutions*, while the correspondences with the Epistle to Barnabas suggest Egypt as the locality. If the *Teaching* and Barnabas have a common basis, e.g., the *Duæ Viæ*, the last may be assigned to Egypt, and the *Teaching*, in its present form, to Syria. The Palestinian origin is urged by those who lay stress upon the absence of Pauline doctrine in the *Teaching* [If meant for catechumens only, this fact is sufficiently accounted for.]

The question is still an open one.

As regards the doctrine, polity, usages, and ethics expressed and implied in the *Teaching*, the reader can judge for himself. The writer is of the opinion that the work represents, on many of these points, only a very small fraction of the Christians during the second century, and that, while it casts some light upon usages of that period, it cannot be regarded as an authoritative witness concerning the universal faith and practice of believers at the date usually assigned to it. The few notices of it, and its early disappearance, confirm this position. The theory of a composite origin also accords with this estimate of the document as a whole.

The version of the *Teaching* here given is that of Professor Isaac H. Hall and Mr. John T. Napier, which first appeared in the *Sunday-School Times* (Philadelphia), April 12, 1884. It is now republished by permission of the editor of that periodical and of the joint authors. A few slight changes have been made, some of them in accordance with suggestions from Professor Hall, others to indicate correspondences with book vii. of *Apostolic Constitutions*.

The division of verses agrees with that of Harnack as given by Schaff. The headings to the chapters have been inserted by the editor. The Scripture references have been selected and verified. The notes have been kept within narrow limits. They serve to indicate the relation of the matter to that in other early writings, mainly the *Apostolic Constitutions*, and to give various readings and renderings. Occasionally explanations and comments have been inserted. In dealing with this, as with most other books, the best method of study is historico-exegetical. To read the book intelligently is better than to read about it. The editor has sought to furnish some help in this method.

---

1. Compare Rev. ii. 2 and 9.
2. In obscure regions such an admission is clearly consistent with apostolic experience. Compare 1 Cor. iv. 16, 17, xi. 34; Gal. iv. 9.
3. Compare 1 John iv. 1; Titus i. 10.

THE DIDACHE : TEACHING OF THE TWELVE APOSTLES

The Lord's Teaching Through the Twelve Apostles to the Nations.

ΔΙΔΑΧΗ
ΤΩΝ ΔΩΔΕΚΑ ΑΠΟΣΤΟΛΩΝ

1

THE TWO WAYS; THE FIRST COMMANDMENT.

There are two Ways, one of Life and one of Death; but there is a great difference between the two Ways.

2. Now the Way of Life is this: First, Thou shalt love God who made thee; secondly, thy neighbor as thyself; and all things whatsoever thou wouldst not have done to thee, neither do thou to another.

3. Now the teaching of these [two] words [of the Lord] is this: Bless those who curse you, and pray for your enemies, and fast for those who persecute you; for what thank is there if ye love those who love you? Do not even Gentiles the same? But love ye those who hate you, and ye shall not have an enemy.

4. Abstain from fleshly and bodily [worldly] lusts. If any one give thee a blow on the right cheek turn to him the other also, and thou shalt be perfect. If any one press thee to go with

him one mile, go with him two; if any one take away thy cloak, give him also thy tunic; if any one take from thee what is thine, ask it not back, as indeed thou canst not.

5. Give to every one that asketh thee, and ask not back, for the Father wills that from our own blessings we should give to all. Blessed is he that gives according to the commandment, for he is guiltless. Woe to him that receives; for if any one receives, having need, he shall be guiltless, but he that has not need shall give account, why he received and for what purpose, and coming into distress he shall be strictly examined concerning his deeds, and he shall not come out thence till he have paid the last farthing.

6. But concerning this also it hath been said, "Let thine alms sweat (drop like sweat) into thy hands till thou know to whom thou shouldst give."

2

THE SECOND COMMANDMENT: GROSS SIN FORBIDDEN.

And the second commandment of the Teaching is:

2. Thou shalt not kill. Thou shalt not commit adultery; thou shalt not corrupt boys; thou shalt not commit fornication. Thou shalt not steal. Thou shalt not use witchcraft; thou shalt not practice sorcery. Thou shalt not procure abortion, nor shalt thou kill the new-born child. Thou shalt not covet thy neighbor's goods.

3. Thou shalt not forswear thyself (swear falsely). Thou shalt not bear false witness. Thou shalt not speak evil; thou shalt not bear malice.

4. Thou shalt not be double-minded nor double-tongued; for duplicity of tongue is a snare of death.

5. Thy speech shall not be false, nor vain, but fulfilled by deed.

6. Thou shalt not be covetous, nor rapacious, nor a

hypocrite, nor malignant, nor haughty. Thou shalt not take evil counsel against thy neighbor.

7. Thou shalt not hate any one, but some thou shalt rebuke and for some thou shalt pray, and some thou shalt love above thine own soul (or, life).

3

OTHER SINS FORBIDDEN.

My child, flee from every evil, and from every thing that is like unto it.

2. Be not prone to anger, for anger leadeth to murder; nor given to party spirit, nor contentious, nor quick-tempered (or, passionate); for from all these things murders are generated.

3. My child, be not lustful, for lust leadeth to fornication; neither be a filthy talker, nor an eager gazer, for from all these are generated adulteries.

4. My child, be not an observer of birds [for divination] for it leads to idolatry; nor a charmer (enchanter), nor an astrologer, nor a purifier (a user of purifications or expiations), nor be thou willing to look on those things; for from all these is generated idolatry.

5. My child, be not a liar, for lying leads to theft; nor

avaricious, nor vainglorious, for from all these things are generated thefts.

6. My child, be not a murmurer, for it leads to blasphemy; neither self-willed (presumptuous), nor evil-minded, for from all these things are generated blasphemies.

7. But be thou meek, for the meek shall inherit the earth.

8. Be thou long-suffering, and merciful, and harmless, and quiet, and good, and trembling continually at the words which thou hast heard.

9. Thou shalt not exalt thyself, nor shalt thou give audacity (presumption) to thy soul. Thy soul shall not be joined to the lofty, but with the just and lowly shalt thou converse.

10. The events that befall thee thou shalt accept as good, knowing that nothing happens without God.

4

VARIOUS PRECEPTS.

My child, thou shalt remember night and day him that speaks to thee the word of God, and thou shalt honor him as the Lord, for where the Lordship is spoken of, there is the Lord.

2. And thou shalt seek out day by day the faces of the saints, that thou mayest rest upon their words.

3. Thou shalt not desire (make) division, but shalt make peace between those at strife. Thou shalt judge justly; thou shalt not respect a person (or, show partiality) in rebuking for transgressions.

4. Thou shalt not be double-minded (doubtful in thy mind) whether it shall be or not.

5. Be not one that stretches out his hands for receiving, but draws them in for giving.

6. If thou hast [anything], thou shalt give with thy hands a ransom for thy sins.

7. Thou shalt not hesitate to give, nor in giving shalt thou murmur, for thou shalt know who is the good recompenser of the reward.

8. Thou shalt not turn away him that needeth, but shalt share all things with thy brother, and shalt not say that they are thine own; for if you are fellow-sharers in that which is imperishable (immortal), how much more in perishable (mortal) things?

9. Thou shalt not take away thy hand from thy son or from thy daughter, but from [their] youth up thou shalt teach [them] the fear of God.

10. Thou shalt not in thy bitterness lay commands on thy man-servant (bondman), or thy maid-servant (bondwoman), who hope in the same God, lest they should not fear Him who is God over [you] both; for He comes not to call [men] according to the outward appearance (condition), but [he comes] on those whom the Spirit has prepared.

11. But ye, bondmen, shall be subject to our (your) masters as to the image of God in reverence (modesty) and fear.

12. Thou shalt hate all hypocrisy, and everything that is not pleasing to the Lord.

13. Thou shalt not forsake the commandments of the Lord, but thou shalt keep what thou hast received, neither adding [thereto] nor taking away [therefrom].

14. In the congregation (in church) thou shalt confess thy transgressions, and thou shalt not come to thy prayer (or, place of prayer) with an evil conscience.

This is the way of life.

5
THE WAY OF DEATH.

But the way of death is this. First of all it is evil and full of curse; murders, adulteries, lusts, fornications, thefts, idolatries, witchcrafts, sorceries, robberies, false-witnessings, hypocrisies, double-heartedness, deceit, pride, wickedness, self-will, covetousness, filthy-talking, jealousy, presumption, haughtiness, boastfulness.

2. Persecutors of the good, hating truth, loving a lie, not knowing the reward of righteousness, not cleaving to that which is good nor to righteous judgment, watchful not for that which is good but for that which is evil; far from whom is meekness and endurance, loving vanity, seeking after reward, not pitying the poor, not toiling with him who is vexed with toil, not knowing Him that made them, murderers of children, destroyers of the handiwork of God, turning away from the needy, vexing the afflicted, advocates of the rich, lawless judges of the poor, wholly sinful.

May ye, children, be delivered from all these.

6
AGAINST FALSE TEACHERS, AND FOOD OFFERED TO IDOLS.

Take heed that no one lead thee astray from this way of teaching, since he teacheth thee apart from God.

2. For if indeed thou art able to bear the whole yoke of the Lord thou shalt be perfect; but if thou art not able, do what thou canst.

3. And as regards food, bear what thou canst, but against idol-offerings be exceedingly on thy guard, for it is a service of dead gods.

7
CONCERNING BAPTISM.

Now concerning baptism, baptize thus: Having first taught all these things, baptize ye into the name of the Father, and of the Son, and of the Holy Spirit, in living water.

2. And if thou hast not living water, baptize into other water; and if thou canst not in cold, then in warm (water).

3. But if thou hast neither, pour [water] thrice upon the head in the name of the Father, and of the Son, and of the Holy Spirit.

4. But before Baptism let the baptizer and the baptized fast, and any others who can; but thou shalt command the baptized to fast for one or two days before.

8
CONCERNING FASTING AND PRAYER (THE LORD'S PRAYER).

Let not your fasts be with the hypocrites, for they fast on the second and fifth day of the week; but ye shall fast on the fourth day, and the preparation day (Friday).

2. Neither pray ye as the hypocrites, but as the Lord commanded in His Gospel, so pray ye: "Our Father, who art in heaven, hallowed be Thy Name. Thy Kingdom come. Thy will be done, as in heaven, so on earth. Give us this day our daily (needful) bread. And forgive us our debt as we also forgive our debtors. And bring us not into temptation, but deliver us from the evil one (or, from evil). For Thine is the power and the glory for ever."

3. Pray thus thrice a day.

9
THE THANKSGIVING (EUCHARIST).

Now as regards the Eucharist (the Thank-offering), give thanks after this manner:

2. First for the cup: "We give thanks to Thee, our Father, for the holy vine of David Thy servant, which thou hast made known to us through Jesus, Thy servant: to Thee be the glory for ever."

3. And for the broken bread: "We give thanks to Thee, our Father, for the life and knowledge which Thou hast made known to us through Jesus, Thy servant: to Thee be the glory for ever.

4. "As this broken bread was scattered upon the mountains and gathered together became one, so let Thy church be gathered together from the ends of the earth into Thy kingdom, for Thine is the glory and the power through Jesus Christ for ever."

5. But let no one eat or drink of your Eucharist, except those baptized into the name of the Lord; for as regards this also the Lord has said: "Give not that which is holy to the dogs."

10

PRAYER AFTER COMMUNION.

Now after being filled, give thanks after this manner:

2. "We thank Thee, Holy Father, for Thy Holy Name, which Thou hast caused to dwell (tabernacle) in our hearts, and for the knowledge and faith and immortality which Thou hast made known to us through Jesus Thy Servant, to Thee be the glory for ever.

3. "Thou, O, Almighty Sovereign, didst make all things for Thy Name's sake; Thou gavest food and drink to men for enjoyment that they might give thanks to Thee; but to us Thou didst freely give spiritual food and drink and eternal life through Thy Servant.

4. "Before all things we give thanks to Thee that Thou art mighty; to Thee be the glory for ever.

5. "Remember, O Lord, Thy Church to deliver her from all evil and to perfect her in Thy love; and gather her together

from the four winds, sanctified for Thy kingdom which Thou didst prepare for her; for Thine is the power and the glory for ever.

6. "Let grace come, and let this world pass away. Hosanna to the God of David. If any one is holy let him come, if any one is not holy let him repent. Maranatha. Amen."

7. But permit the Prophets to give thanks as much as [in what words] they wish.

11

CONCERNING TEACHERS, APOSTLES, AND PROPHETS.

Whosoever then comes and teaches you all the things aforesaid, receive him.

2. But if the teacher himself being perverted teaches another teaching to the destruction [of this], hear him not, but if [he teach] to the increase of righteousness and the knowledge of the Lord, receive him as the Lord.

3. Now with regard to the Apostles and Prophets, according to the decree (command) of the gospel, so do ye.

4. Let every Apostle that cometh to you be received as the Lord.

5. But he shall not remain [longer than] one day; and, if need be, another [day] also; but if he remain three [days] he is a false prophet.

6. And when the Apostle departeth, let him take nothing except bread [enough] till he reach his lodging (night-quarters). But if he ask for money, he is a false prophet.

7. And every prophet who speaks in the spirit ye shall not try or prove; for every sin shall be forgiven, but this sin shall not be forgiven.

8. Not every one that speaks in the spirit is a Prophet, but only if he has the behavior (the ways) of the Lord. By their behavior then shall the false prophet and the [true] Prophet be known.

9. And no Prophet that orders a table in the spirit eats of it [himself], unless he is a false prophet.

10. And every Prophet who teaches the truth if he does not practice what he teaches, is a false prophet.

11. And every approved, genuine Prophet, who makes assemblies for a worldly mystery, but does not teach [others] to do what he himself does, shall not be judged by you; for he has his judgment with God (or, his judgment is in the hands of God); for so did also the ancient Prophets.

12. But whosoever says in the spirit: Give me money or any other thing, ye shall not listen to him; but if he bid you to give for others that lack, let no one judge him.

12

RECEPTION OF CHRISTIANS.

Let every one that comes in the name of the Lord be received, and then proving him ye shall know him; for ye shall have understanding right and left.

2. If indeed he who comes is a wayfarer, help him as much as ye can; but he shall not remain with you longer than two or three days, unless there be necessity.

3. If he wishes to settle among you, being a craftsman (artisan), let him work and eat (earn his living by work).

4. But if he has not handicraft (trade), provide according to your understanding that no Christian shall live idle among you.

5. And if he will not act thus he is a Christ-trafficker. Beware of such.

13
SUPPORT OF PROPHETS.

But every true Prophet who wishes to settle among you is worthy of his food (or, support).

2. Likewise a true Teacher is himself worthy, like the workman, of his food.

3. Therefore thou shalt take and give all the first-fruit of the produce of the wine-press and threshing-floor, of oxen and sheep, to the Prophets; for they are your chief-priests.

4. But if ye have no Prophet, give to the poor.

5. If thou preparest bread, take the first fruit and give according to the commandment.

6. Likewise when thou openest a jar of wine or of oil, take the first-fruit and give to the Prophets.

7. And of silver, and raiment, and every possession, take the first-fruit, as may seem good to thee, and give according to the commandment.

14

CHRISTIAN ASSEMBLY ON THE LORD'S DAY.

And on the Lord's Day of the Lord come together, and break bread, and give thanks, having before confessed your transgressions, that your sacrifice may be pure.

2. Let no one who has a dispute with his fellow come together with you until they are reconciled, that your sacrifice may not be defiled.

3. For this is that which was spoken by the Lord: "In every place and time offer me a pure sacrifice, for I am a great King, saith the Lord, and my name is wonderful among the Gentiles."

15

BISHOPS AND DEACONS; CHRISTIAN REPROOF.

Elect therefore for yourselves Bishops and Deacons worthy of the Lord, men meek, and not lovers of money, and truthful, and approved; for they too minister to you the ministry of the Prophets and Teachers.

2. Therefore despise them not, for they are those that are the honored [men] among you with the Prophets and Teachers.

3. And reprove one another not in wrath, but in peace, as ye have [it] in the gospel; and with every one that transgresses against another let no one speak, nor let him hear [a word] from you until he repents.

4. But so do your prayers and alms and all your actions as ye have [it] in the gospel of our Lord.

16

WATCHFULNESS; THE COMING OF THE LORD.

Watch over your life; let not your lamps be quenched and let not your loins be unloosed, but be ye ready; for ye know not the hour in which our Lord comes.

2. But be ye frequently gathered together, seeking the things that are profitable for your souls; for the whole time of your faith shall not profit you except in the last season ye be found perfect.

3. For in the last days the false prophets and destroyers shall be multiplied, and the sheep shall be turned into wolves, and love shall be turned into hate.

4. For when lawlessness increases, they shall hate and persecute, and deliver up one another; and then shall appear the world-deceiver as Son of God, and shall do signs and wonders, and the earth shall be delivered into his hands, and

he shall commit iniquities which have never yet come to pass from the beginning of the world.

5. And then shall the race of men come into the fire of trial, and many shall be offended and shall perish; but they who endure in their faith shall be saved from under the curse itself.

6. And then shall appear the signs of the truth: first the sign of opening in heaven; then the sign of the voice of the trumpet; and the third, the resurrection of the dead.

7. Not, however, of all, but as was said, "The Lord shall come, and all the saints with him."

8. Then shall the world see the Lord coming upon the clouds of heaven.

THE EPISTLE OF BARNABAS

INTRODUCTORY NOTE TO THE EPISTLE OF BARNABAS

The writer of this Epistle is supposed to have been an Alexandrian Jew of the times of Trajan and Hadrian. He was a layman; but possibly he bore the name of "Barnabas," and so has been confounded with his holy and apostolic name-sire. It is more probable that the Epistle, being anonymous, was attributed to St. Barnabas, by those who supposed that apostle to be the author of the Epistle to the Hebrews, and who discovered similarities in the plan and purpose of the two works. It is with great reluctance that I yield to modern scholars, in dismissing the ingenious and temperate argument of Archbishop Wake[1] for the apostolic origin of this treatise. The learned Lardner[2] shares his convictions; and the very interesting and ingenious views of Jones[3] never appeared to me satisfactory, weighed with preponderating arguments, on the other side.[4]

The Maccabæan spirit of the Jews never burned more furiously than after the destruction of Jerusalem, and while it was kindling the conflagration that broke out under Barchochebas, and blazed so terribly in the insurrection against Hadrian.[5] It is not credible that the Jewish Christians at Alexandria and elsewhere were able to emancipate themselves from their national spirit; and accordingly the old Judaizing, which St. Paul had anathematized and confuted, would assert itself again. If such was the occasion of this Epistle, as I venture to suppose, a higher character must be ascribed to it than could otherwise be claimed. This accounts, also, for the degree of favour with which it was accepted by the primitive faithful.

It is interesting as a specimen of their conflicts with a persistent Judaism which St. Paul had defeated and anathematized, but which was ever cropping out among believers originally of the Hebrews.[6] Their own habits of allegorizing, and their Oriental tastes, must be borne in mind, if we are readily disgusted with our author's fancies and refinements. St. Paul himself pays a practical tribute to their modes of thought, in his Epistle to the Galatians iv. 24. This is the *ad hominem* form of rhetoric, familiar to all speakers, which laid even the apostle open to the slander of enemies (2 Cor. xii. 16),—that he was "crafty," and caught men with guile. It is interesting to note the more Occidental spirit of Cyprian, as compared with our author, when he also contends with Judaism. Doubtless we have in the pseudo-Barnabas something of that *œconomy* which is always capable of abuse, and which was destined too soon to overleap the bounds of its moral limitations.

It is to be observed that this writer sometimes speaks as a

Gentile, a fact which some have found it difficult to account for, on the supposition that he was a Hebrew, if not a Levite as well. But so, also, St. Paul sometimes speaks as a Roman, and sometimes as a Jew; and, owing to the mixed character of the early Church, he writes to the Romans iv. 1 as if they were all Israelites, and again to the same Church (Rom. xi. 13) as if they were all Gentiles. So this writer sometimes identifies himself with Jewish thought as a son of Abraham, and again speaks from the Christian position as if he were a Gentile, thus identifying himself with the catholicity of the Church.

But the subject thus opened is vast; and "the Epistle of Barnabas," so called, still awaits a critical editor, who at the same time shall be a competent expositor. Nobody can answer these requisitions, who is unable, for this purpose, to be a Christian of the days of Trajan.

But it will be observed that this version has great advantages over any of its predecessor, and is a valuable acquisition to the student. The learned translators have had before them the entire Greek text of the fourth century, disfigured is true by corruptions, but still very precious, the rather as they have been able to compare it with the text of Hilgenfeld. Their editorial notes are sufficient for our own plan; and little has been left for me to do, according to the scheme of this publication, save to revise the "copy" for printing. I am glad to presume no further into such a labyrinth, concerning which the learned and careful Wake modestly professes, "I have endeavoured to attain to the sense of my author, and to make him as plain and easy as I was able. If in anything I have chanced to mistake him, I have only this to say for myself: that he must be better acquainted with the road than I pretend to be, who will undertake to travel so long a journey in the dark and never to miss his way."

～

The following is the original Introductory Notice:—

Nothing certain is known as to the author of the following Epistle. The writer's name is Barnabas, but scarcely any scholars now ascribe it to the illustrious friend and companion of St. Paul. External and internal evidence here come into direct collision. The ancient writers who refer to this Epistle unanimously attribute it to Barnabas the Levite, of Cyprus, who held such an honourable place in the infant Church. Clement of Alexandria does so again and again (*Strom.*, ii. 6, ii. 7, etc.). Origen describes it as "a Catholic Epistle" (*Cont. Cels.*, i. 63), and seems to rank it among the Sacred Scriptures (*Comm. in Rom.*, i. 24). Other statements have been quoted from the fathers, to show that they held this to be an authentic production of the apostolic Barnabas; and certainly no other name is ever hinted at in Christian antiquity as that of the writer. But notwithstanding this, the internal evidence is now generally regarded as conclusive against this opinion. On perusing the Epistle, the reader will be in circumstances to judge of this matter for himself. He will be led to consider whether the spirit and tone of the writing, as so decidedly opposed to all respect for Judaism—the numerous inaccuracies which it contains with respect to Mosaic enactments and observances —the absurd and trifling interpretations of Scripture which it suggests—and the many silly vaunts of superior knowledge in which its writer indulges—can possibly comport with its ascription to the fellow—labourer of St. Paul. When it is remembered that no one ascribes the Epistle to the apostolic Barnabas till the times of Clement of Alexandria, and that it is ranked by Eusebius among the "spurious" writings, which, however much known and read in the Church, were never regarded as authoritative, little doubt can remain that the external evidence is of itself weak, and should not make us hesitate for a moment in refusing to ascribe this writing to Barnabas the Apostle.

The date, object, and intended reader of the Epistle can only be doubtfully inferred from some statements which it contains. It was clearly written after the destruction of Jerusalem, since reference is made to that event (chap. xvi.), but how long after is matter of much dispute. The general opinion is, that its date is not later than the middle of the second century, and that it cannot be placed earlier than some twenty or thirty years before. In point of style, both as respects thought and expression, a very low place must be assigned it. We know nothing certain of the region in which the author lived, or where the first readers were to be found. The intention of the writer, as he himself states (chap. i), was "to perfect the knowledge" of those to whom he wrote. Hilgenfeld, who has devoted much attention to this Epistle, holds that "it was written at the close of the first century by a Gentile Christian of the school of Alexandria, with the view of winning back, or guarding from a Judaic form of Christianity, those Christians belonging to the same class as himself."

Until the recent discovery of the Codex Sinaiticus by Tischendorf, the first four and a half chapters were known only in an ancient Latin version. The whole Greek text is now happily recovered, though it is in many places very corrupt. We have compared its readings throughout, and noted the principal variations from the text represented in our version. We have also made frequent reference to the text adopted by Hilgenfeld in his recent edition of the Epistle (Lipsiæ, T. O. Weigel, 1886).

---

1. Discourse (p. 148) to his *Genuine* Epistles of the Apostolical Fathers. *Philadelphia, 1846.*
2. Works, ii. 250, note; and iv. 128.
3. *On the Canon*, vol. ii. p. 431.
4. To those who may adhere to the older opinion, let me commend the eloquent and instructive chapter (xxiii.) in Farrar's *Life of St. Paul.*
5. Hadrian's purpose to rebuild their city seems to be pointed out in chap. xvi.
6. M. Renan may be read with pain, and yet with profit, in much that his Gallio-spirit suggests on this subject. Chap. v., *St. Paul*, Paris, 1884.

1

AFTER THE SALUTATION, THE WRITER DECLARES THAT HE WOULD COMMUNICATE TO HIS BRETHREN SOMETHING OF THAT WHICH HE HAD HIMSELF RECEIVED.

All hail, ye sons and daughters, in the name of our Lord Jesus Christ, who loved us in peace.

Seeing that the divine fruits of righteousness abound among you, I rejoice exceedingly and above measure in your happy and honoured spirits, because ye have with such effect received the engrafted spiritual gift. Wherefore also I inwardly rejoice the more, hoping to be saved, because I truly perceive in you the Spirit poured forth from the rich Lord s of love. Your greatly desired appearance has thus filled me with astonishment over you. I am therefore pursuaded of this, and fully convinced in my own mind, that since I began to speak among you I understand many things, because the Lord hath accompanied me in the way of righteousness. I am also on this account bound by the strictest obligation to love you above my own soul, because great are the faith and love dwelling in you, while you hope for the life which He has promised. Considering this, therefore, that if I should take the trouble to communicate to you some portion of what I have myself received, it will prove to me a sufficient reward that I minister to such spirits, I have hastened briefly to write unto you, in order that, along with your faith, ye might have perfect knowledge. The doctrines of the Lord, then, are three: the hope of life, the beginning and the completion of it. For the Lord hath made known to us by the prophets both the things which are past and present, giving us also the first-fruits of the knowledge of things to come, which things as we see accomplished, one by one, we ought with the greater richness of faith and elevation of spirit to draw near to Him with reverence. I then, not as your teacher, but as one of yourselves, will set forth a few things by which in present circumstances ye may be rendered the more joyful.

2

THE JEWISH SACRIFICES ARE NOW ABOLISHED.

Since, therefore, the days are evil, and Satan possesses the power of this world, we ought to give heed to ourselves, and diligently inquire into the ordinances of the Lord. Fear and patience, then, are helpers of our faith; and long-suffering and continence are things which fight on our side. While these remain pure in what respects the Lord, Wisdom, Understanding, Science, and Knowledge rejoice along with them. For He hath revealed to us by all the prophets that He needs neither sacrifices, nor burnt-offerings, nor oblations, saying thus, "What is the multitude of your sacrifices unto Me, saith the Lord? I am full of burnt-offerings, and desire not the fat of lambs, and the blood of bulls and goats, not when ye come to appear before Me: for who hath required these things at your hands? Tread no more My courts, not though ye bring with you fine flour. Incense is a vain abomination unto Me, and your new moons and sabbaths I cannot endure." He has therefore abolished these things, that the new law of our Lord Jesus Christ, which is without the yoke of necessity, might have a human oblation. And again He says to them, "Did I command your fathers, when they went out from the land of Egypt, to offer unto Me burnt-offerings and sacrifices? But this rather I commanded them, Let no one of you cherish any evil in his heart against his neighbour, and love not an oath of falsehood." We ought therefore, being possessed of understanding, to perceive the gracious intention of our Father; for He speaks to us, desirous that we, not going astray like them, should ask how we may approach Him. To us, then, He declares, "A sacrifice [pleasing] to God is a broken spirit; a smell of sweet savour to the Lord is a heart that glorifieth Him that made it." We ought therefore, brethren, carefully to inquire concerning our salvation, lest the wicked one, having made his entrance by deceit, should huff us forth from our [true] life.

3
THE FASTS OF THE JEWS ARE NOT TRUE FASTS, NOR ACCEPTABLE TO GOD.

He says then to them again concerning these things, "Why do ye fast to Me as on this day, saith the Lord, that your voice should be heard with a cry? I have not chosen this fast, saith the Lord, that a man should humble his soul. Nor, though ye bend your neck like a ring, and put upon you sackcloth and ashes, will ye call it an acceptable fast." To us He saith, "Behold, this is the fast that I have chosen, saith the Lord, not that a man should humble his soul, but that he should loose every band of iniquity, untie the fastenings of harsh agreements, restore to liberty them that are bruised, tear in pieces every unjust engagement, feed the hungry with thy bread, clothe the naked when thou seest him, bring the homeless into thy house, not despise the humble if thou behold him, and not [turn away] from the members of thine own family. Then shall thy dawn break forth, and thy healing shall quickly spring up, and righteousness shall go forth before thee, and the glory of God shall encompass thee; and then thou shalt call, and God shall hear thee; whilst thou art yet speaking, He shall say, Behold, I am with thee; if thou take away from thee the chain [binding others], and the stretching forth of the hands [to sweat falsely], and words of murmuring, and give cheerfully thy bread to the hungry, and show compassion to the soul that has been humbled." To this end, therefore, brethren, He is long-suffering, foreseeing how the people whom He has prepared shall with guilelessness believe in His Beloved. For He revealed all these things to us beforehand, that we should not rush forward as rash acceptors of their laws.

4
ANTICHRIST IS AT HAND: LET US THEREFORE AVOID JEWISH ERRORS.

It therefore behoves us, who inquire much concerning events at hand, to search diligently into those things which are able to save us. Let us then utterly flee from all the works of iniquity, lest these should take hold of us; and let us hate the error of the present time, that we may set our love on the world to come: let us not give loose reins to our soul, that it should have power to run with sinners and the wicked, lest we become like them. The final stumbling-block (or source of danger) approaches, concerning which it is written, as Enoch says, "For for this end the Lord has cut short the times and the days, that His Beloved may hasten; and He will come to the inheritance." And the prophet also speaks thus: "Ten kingdoms shall reign upon the earth, and a little king shall rise up after them, who shall subdue under one three of the kings. In like manner Daniel says concerning the same, "And I beheld the fourth beast, wicked and powerful, and more savage than all the beasts of the earth, and how from it sprang up ten horns, and out of them a little budding horn, and how it subdued under one three of the great horns." Ye ought therefore to understand. And this also I further beg of you, as being one of you, and loving you both individually and collectively more than my own soul, to take heed now to yourselves, and not to be like some, adding largely to your sins, and saying, "The covenant is both theirs and ours." But they thus finally lost it, after Moses had already received it. For the Scripture saith, "And Moses was fasting in the mount forty days and forty nights, and received the covenant from the Lord, tables of stone written with the finger of the hand of the Lord;" but turning away to idols, they lost it. For the Lord speaks thus to Moses: "Moses go down quickly; for the people whom thou hast brought out of the land of Egypt have transgressed." And Moses understood [the meaning of God], and cast the two tables out of his hands; and their covenant was broken, in order that the covenant of the beloved Jesus might be sealed upon our heart, in the hope which flows from believing in Him. Now, being desirous to write many things to you, not as your teacher, but as becometh one who loves you, I have taken care not to fail to write to you from what I myself possess, with a view to your purification. We take earnest heed in these last days; for the whole [past] time of your faith will profit you nothing, unless now in this wicked time we also withstand coming sources of danger, as becometh the sons of God. That the Black One may find no means of entrance, let us flee from every vanity, let us utterly hate the works of the way of wickedness. Do not, by retiring apart, live a solitary life, as if you were already [fully] justified; but coming together in one place, make common inquiry concerning what tends to your general welfare. For the Scripture saith, "Woe to them who are wise to themselves, and prudent in their own sight!" Let us be spiritually-minded: let us be a perfect temple to God. As much as in us lies, let us meditate upon the fear of God, and let us keep His commandments, that we may rejoice in His ordinances. The Lord will judge the world without respect of persons. Each will receive as he has done: if he is righteous, his righteousness will precede him; if he is wicked, the reward of wickedness is before him. Take heed, lest resting at our ease, as those who are the called [of God], we should fall asleep in our sins, and the wicked prince, acquiring power over us, should thrust us away from the kingdom of the Lord. And all the more attend to this, my brethren, when ye reflect and behold, that after so great signs and wonders were wrought in Israel, they were thus [at length] abandoned. Let us beware lest we be found [fulfilling that saying], as it is written, "Many are called, but few are chosen."

5
THE NEW COVENANT, FOUNDED ON THE SUFFERINGS OF CHRIST, TENDS TO OUR SALVATION, BUT TO THE JEWS' DESTRUCTION.

For to this end the Lord endured to deliver up His flesh to corruption, that we might be sanctified through the remission of sins, which is effected by His blood of sprinkling. For it is written concerning Him, partly with reference to Israel, and partly to us; and [the Scripture] saith thus: "He was wounded for our transgressions, and braised for our iniquities: with His stripes we are healed. He was brought as a sheep to the slaughter, and as a lamb which is dumb before its shearer." Therefore we ought to be deeply grateful to the Lord, because He has both made known to us things that are past, and hath given us wisdom concerning things present, and hath not left us without understanding in regard to things which are to come. Now, the Scripture saith, "Not unjustly are nets spread out for birds." This means that the man perishes justly, who, having a knowledge of the way of righteousness, rushes off into the way of darkness. And further, my brethren: if the Lord endured to suffer for our soul, He being Lord of all the world, to whom God said at the foundation of the world, "Let us make man after our image, and after our likeness," understand how it was that He endured to suffer at the hand of men. The prophets, having obtained grace from Him, prophesied concerning Him. And He (since it behoved Him to appear in flesh), that He might abolish death, and reveal the resurrection from the dead, endured [what and as He did], in order that He might fulfill the promise made unto the fathers, and by preparing a new people for Himself, might show, while He dwelt on earth, that He, when He has raised mankind, will also judge them. Moreover, teaching Israel, and doing so great miracles and signs, He preached [the truth] to him, and greatly loved him. But when He chose His own apostles who where to preach His Gospel, [He did so from among those] who were sinners above all sin, that He might show He came "not to call the righteous, but sinners to repentance." Then He manifested Himself to be the Son of God. For if He had not come in the flesh, how could men have been saved by beholding Him? Since looking upon the sun which is to cease to exist, and is the work of His hands, their eyes are not able to bear his rays. The Son of God therefore came in the flesh with this view, that He might bring to a head the sum of their sins who had persecuted His prophets to the death. For this purpose, then, He endured. For God saith, "The stroke of his flesh is from them;" and "when I shall smite the Shepherd, then the sheep of the flock shall be scattered." He himself willed thus to suffer, for it was necessary that He should suffer on the tree. For says he Who prophesies regarding Him, "Spare my soul from the sword, fasten my flesh with nails; for the assemblies of the wicked have risen up against me." And again he says, "Behold, I have given my back to scourges, and my cheeks to strokes, and I have set my countenance as a firm rock."

6

THE SUFFERINGS OF CHRIST, AND THE NEW COVENANT, WERE ANNOUNCED BY THE PROPHETS.

When, therefore, He has fulfilled the commandment, what saith He? "Who is he that will contend with Me? let him oppose Me: or who is he that will enter into judgment with Me? let him draw near to the servant of the Lord." "Woe unto you, for ye shall all wax old, like a garment, and the moth shall eat you up." And again the prophet says, "Since as a mighty stone He is laid for crushing, behold I cast down for the foundations of Zion a stone, precious, elect, a corner-stone, honourable." Next, what says He? "And he who shall trust" in it shall live for ever." Is our hope, then, upon a stone? Far from it. But [the language is used] inasmuch as He laid his flesh [as a foundation] with power; for He says, "And He placed me as a firm rock." And the prophet says again, "The stone which the builders rejected, the same has become the head of the corner." And again he says, "This is the great and wonderful day which the Lord hath made. I write the more simply unto you, that ye may understand. I am the off-scouring of your love. What, then, again says the prophet? "The assembly of the wicked surrounded me; they encompassed me as bees do a honeycomb," and "upon my garment they cast lots." Since, therefore, He was about to be manifested and to suffer in the flesh, His suffering was foreshown. For the prophet speaks against Israel, "Woe to their soul, because they have counselted an evil counsel against themselves, saying, Let us bind the just one, because he is displeasing to us." And Moses also says to them, "Behold these things, saith the Lord God: Enter into the good land which the Lord sware [to give] to Abraham, and Isaac, and Jacob, and inherit ye it, a land flowing with milk and honey." What, then, says Knowledge? Learn: "Trust," she says, "in Him who is to be manifested to you in the flesh--that is, Jesus." For man is earth in a suffering state, for the formation of Adam was from the face of the earth. What, then, meaneth this: "into the good land, a land flowing with milk and honey?" Blessed be our Lord, who has placed in us wisdom and understanding of secret things. For the prophet says, "Who shall understand the parable of the Lord, except him who is wise and prudent, and who loves his Lord?" Since, therefore, having renewed us by the remission of our sins, He hath made us after another pattern, [it is His purpose] that we should possess the soul of children, inasmuch as He has created us anew by His Spirit. For the Scripture says concerning us, while He speaks to the Son, "Let Us make man after Our image, and after Our likeness; and let them have dominion over the beasts of the earth, and the fowls of heaven, and the fishes of the sea." And the Lord said, on beholding the fair creature man, "Increase, and multiply, and replenish the earth." These things [were spoken] to the Son. Again, I will show thee how, in respect to us, He has accomplished a second fashioning in these last days. The Lord says, "Behold, I will make the last like the first." In reference to this, then, the prophet proclaimed, "Enter ye into the land flowing with milk and honey, and have dominion over it." Behold, therefore, we have been refashioned, as again He says in another prophet, "Behold, saith the Lord, I will take away from these, that is, from those whom the Spirit of the Lord foresaw, their stony hearts, and I will put hearts of flesh within them," because He was to be manifested in flesh, and to sojourn among us. For, my brethren, the habitation of our heart is a holy temple to the Lord. For again saith the Lord, "And wherewith shall I appear before the Lord my God, and be glorified?" He says, "I will confess to thee in the Church in the midst of my brethren; and I will praise thee in the midst of the assembly of the saints." We, then, are they whom He has led into the good land. What, then, mean milk and honey? This, that as the infant is kept alive first by honey, and then by milk, so also we, being quickened and kept alive by the faith of the promise and by the word, shall live ruling over the earth. But He said above, "Let them increase, and nile over the fishes." Who then is able to govern the beasts, or the fishes, or the fowls of heaven? For we ought to perceive that to govern implies authority, so that one should command and rule. If, therefore, this does not exist at present, yet still He has promised it to us. When? When we ourselves also have been made perfect [so as] to become heirs of the covenant of the Lord."

7
FASTING, AND THE GOAT SENT AWAY, WERE TYPES OF CHRIST.

Understand, then, ye children of gladness, that the good Lord has foreshown all things to us, that we might know to whom we ought for everything to render thanksgiving and praise. If therefore the Son of God, who is Lord all things], and who will judge the living and the dead, suffered, that His stroke might give us life, let us believe that the Son of God could not have suffered except for our sakes. Moreover, when fixed to the cross, He had given Him to drink vinegar and gall. Hearken how the priests of the people gave previous indications of this. His commandment having been written, the Lord enjoined, that whosoever did not keep the fast should be put to death, because He also Himself was to offer in sacrifice for our sins the vessel of the Spirit, in order that the type established in Isaac when he was offered upon the altar might be fully accomplished. What, then, says He in the prophet? "And let them eat of the goat which is offered, with fasting, for all their sins." Attend carefully: "And let all the priests alone eat the inwards, unwashed with vinegar." Wherefore? Because to me, who am to offer my flesh for the sins of my new people, ye are to give gall with vinegar to drink: eat ye alone, while the people fast and mourn in sackcloth and ashes. [These things were done] that He might show that it was necessary for Him to suffer for them. How, then, ran the commandment? Give your attention. Take two goats of goodly aspect, and similar to each other, and offer them. And let the priest take one as a burnt-offering for sins. And what should they do with the other? "Accursed," says He, "is the one." Mark how the type of Jesus now comes out. "And all of you spit upon it, and pierce it, and encircle its head with scarlet wool, and thus let it be driven into the wilderness." And when all this has been done, he who bears the goat brings it into the desert, and takes the wool off from it, and places that upon a shrub which is called Rachia, of which also we are accustomed to eat the fruits when we find them in the field. Of this kind of shrub alone the fruits are sweet. Why then, again, is this? Give good heed. [You see] "one upon the altar, and the other accursed;" and why [do you behold] the one that is accursed crowned? Because they shall see Him then in that day having a scarlet robe about his body down to his feet; and they shall say, Is not this He whom we once despised, and pierced, and mocked, and crucified? Truly this is He who then declared Himself to be the Son of God. For how like is He to Him! With a view to this, [He required] the goats to be of goodly aspect, and similar, that, when they see Him then coming, they may be amazed by the likeness of the goat. Behold, then, the type of Jesus who was to suffer. But why is it that they place the wool in the midst of thorns? It is a type of Jesus set before the view of the Church. [They place the wool among thorns], that any one who wishes to bear it away may find it necessary to suffer much, because the thorn is formidable, and thus obtain it only as the result of suffering. Thus also, says He, "Those who wish to behold Me, and lay hold of My kingdom, must through tribulation and suffering obtain Me."

8

THE RED HEIFER A TYPE OF CHRIST.

Now what do you suppose this to be a type of, that a command was given to Israel, that men of the greatest wickedness should offer a heifer, and slay and burn it, and, that then boys should take the ashes, and put these into vessels, and bind round a stick purple wool along with hyssop, and that thus the boys should sprinkle the people, one by one, in order that they might be purified from their sins? Consider how He speaks to you with simplicity. The calf is Jesus: the sinful men offering it are those who led Him to the slaughter. But now the men are no longer guilty, are no longer regarded as sinners. And the boys that sprinkle are those that have proclaimed to us the remission of sins and purification of heart. To these He gave authority to preach the Gospel, being twelve in number, corresponding to the twelve tribes of Israel. But why are there three boys that sprinkle? To correspond to Abraham, and Isaac, and Jacob, because these were great with God. And why was the wool [placed] upon the wood? Because by wood Jesus holds His kingdom, so that [through the cross] those believing on Him shall live for ever. But why was hyssop joined with the wool? Because in His kingdom the days will be evil and polluted in which we shall be saved, [and] because he who suffers in body is cured through the cleansing efficacy of hyssop. And on this account the things which stand thus are clear to us, but obscure to them because they did not hear the voice of the Lord.

9
THE SPIRITUAL MEANING OF CIRCUMCISION.

He speaks moreover concerning our ears, how He hath circumcised both them and our heart. The Lord saith in the prophet, "In the hearing of the ear they obeyed me." And again He saith, "By hearing, those shall hear who are afar off; they shall know what I have done." And, "Be ye circumcised in your hearts, saith the Lord." And again He says, "Hear, O Israel, for these things saith the Lord thy God." And once more the Spirit of the Lord proclaims, "Who is he that wishes to live for ever? By hearing let him hear the voice of my servant." And again He saith, "Hear, O heaven, and give ear, O earth, for God hath spoken." These are in proof. And again He saith, "Hear the word of the Lord, ye rulers of this people." And again He saith, "Hear, ye children, the voice of one crying in the wilderness." Therefore He hath circumcised our ears, that we might hear His word and believe, for the circumcision in which they trusted is abolished. For He declared that circumcision was not of the flesh, but they transgressed because an evil angel deluded them. He saith to them, "These things saith the Lord your God"-(here I find a new commandment)--"Sow not among thorns, but circumcise yourselves to the Lord." And why speaks He thus: "Circumcise the stubbornness of your heart, and harden not your neck?" And again: "Behold, saith the Lord, all the nations are uncircumcised in the flesh, but this people are uncircumcised in heart." But thou wilt say, "Yea, verily the people are circumcised for a seal." But so also is every Syrian and Arab, and all the priests of idols: are these then also within the bond of His covenant? Yea, the Egyptians also practise circumcision. Learn then, my children, con cerning all things richly, that Abraham, the first who enjoined circumcision, looking forward in spirit to Jesus, practised that rite, having received the mysteries of the three letters. For [the Scripture] saith, "And Abraham circumcised ten, and eight, and three hundred men of his household." What, then, was the knowledge given to him in this? Learn the eighteen first, and then the three hundred. The ten and the eight are thus denoted--Ten by I, and Eight by H. You have [the initials of the, name of] Jesus. And because the cross was to express the grace [of our redemption] by the letter The says also, "Three Hundred." He signifies, therefore, Jesus by two letters, and the cross by one. He knows this, who has put within us the engrafted gift of His doctrine. No one has been admitted by me to a more excellent piece of knowledge than this, but I know that ye are worthy.

10

SPIRITUAL SIGNIFICANCE OF THE PRECEPTS OF MOSES RESPECTING DIFFERENT KINDS OF FOOD.

Now, wherefore did Moses say, "Thou shalt not eat the swine, nor the eagle, nor the hawk, nor the raven, nor any fish which is not possessed of scales?" He embraced three doctrines in his mind [in doing so]. Moreover, the Lord saith to them in Deuteronomy, "And I will establish my ordinances among this people." Is there then not a command of God they should not eat [these things]? There is, but Moses spoke with a spiritual reference. For this reason he named the swine, as much as to say, "Thou shalt not join thyself to men who resemble swine." For when they live in pleasure, they forget their Lord; but when they come to want, they acknowledge the Lord. And [in like manner] the swine, when it has eaten, does not recognize its master; but when hungry it cries out, and on receiving food is quiet again. "Neither shalt thou eat," says he "the eagle, nor the hawk, nor the kite, nor the raven." "Thou shalt not join thyself," he means, "to such men as know not how to procure food for themselves by labour and sweat, but seize on that of others in their iniquity, and although wearing an aspect of simplicity, are on the watch to plunder others." So these birds, while they sit idle, inquire how they may devour the flesh of others, proving themselves pests [to all] by their wickedness. "And thou shalt not eat," he says, "the lamprey, or the polypus, or the cuttlefish." He means, "Thou shalt not join thyself or be like to such men as are ungodly to the end, and are condemned to death." In like manner as those fishes, above accursed, float in the deep, not swimming [on the surface] like the rest, but make their abode in the mud which lies at the bottom. Moreover, "Thou shall not," he says, "eat the hare." Wherefore? "Thou shall not be a corrupter of boys, nor like unto such." Because the hare multiplies, year by year, the places of its conception; for as many years as it lives so many it has. Moreover, "Thou shall not eat the hyena." He means, "Thou shall not be an adulterer, nor a corrupter, nor be like to them that are such." Wherefore? Because that animal annually changes its sex, and is at one time male, and at another female. Moreover, he has rightly detested the weasel. For he means, "Thou shalt not be like to those whom we hear of as committing wickedness with the mouth, on account of their uncleanness; nor shall thou be joined to those impure women who commit iniquity with the mouth. For this animal conceives by the mouth." Moses then issued three doctrines concerning meats with a spiritual significance; but they received them according to fleshly desire, as if he had merely spoken of [literal] meats.

David, however, comprehends the knowledge of the three doctrines, and speaks in like manner: "Blessed is the man who hath not walked in the counsel of the ungodly," even as the fishes [referred to] go in darkness to the depths [of the sea]; "and hath not stood in the way of sinners," even as those who profess to fear the Lord, but go astray like swine; "and hath not sat in the seat of scorners," even as those birds that lie in wait for prey. Take a full and firm grasp of this spiritual knowledge. But Moses says still further, "Ye shall eat every animal that is cloven-footed and ruminant." What does he mean? [The ruminant animal denotes him] who, on receiving food, recognizes Him that nourishes him, and being satisfied by Him, is visibly made glad. Well spake [Moses], having respect to the commandment. What, then, does he mean? That we ought to join ourselves to those that fear the Lord, those who meditate in their heart on the commandment which they have received, those who both utter the judgments of the Lord and observe them, those who know that meditation is a work of gladness, and who ruminate upon the word of the Lord. But what means the cloven-footed? That the righteous man also walks in this world, yet looks forward to the holy state [to come]. Behold how well Moses legislated. But how was it possible for them to understand or comprehend these things? We then, rightly understanding his commandments, explain them as the Lord intended. For this purpose He circumcised our ears and our hearts, that we might understand these things.

11

BAPTISM AND THE CROSS PREFIGURED IN THE OLD TESTAMENT.

Let us further inquire whether the Lord took any care to foreshadow the water [of baptism] and the cross. Concerning the water, indeed, it is written, in reference to the Israelites, that they should not receive that baptism which leads to the remission of sins, but should procure another for themselves. The prophet therefore declares, "Be astonished, O heaven, and let the earth tremble at this, because this people hath committed two great evils: they have forsaken Me, a living fountain, and have hewn out for themselves broken cisterns. Is my holy hill Zion a desolate rock? For ye shall be as the fledglings of a bird, which fly away when the nest is removed." And again saith the prophet, "I will go before thee and make level the mountains, and will break the brazen gates, and bruise in pieces the iron bars; and I will give thee the secret,s hidden, invisible treasures, that they may know that I am the Lord God." And "He shall dwell in a lofty cave of the strong rock." Furthermore, what saith He in reference to the Son? "His water is sure; ye shall see the King in His glory, and your soul shall meditate on the fear of the Lord." And again He saith in another prophet, "The man who doeth these things shall be like a tree planted by the courses of waters, which shall yield its fruit in due season; and his leaf shall not fade, and all that he doeth shall prosper. Not so are the ungodly, not so, but even as chaff, which the wind sweeps away from the face of the earth. Therefore the ungodly shall not stand in judgment, nor sinners in the counsel of the just; for the Lord knoweth the way of the righteous, but the way of the ungodly shall perish." Mark how He has described at once both the water and the cross. For these words imply, Blessed are they who, placing their trust in the cross, have gone down into the water; for, says He, they shall receive their reward in due time: then He declares, I will recompense them. But now He saith, "Their leaves shall not fade." This meaneth, that every word which proceedeth out of your mouth in faith and love shall tend to bring conversion and hope to many. Again, another prophet saith, "And the land of Jacob shall be extolled above every land." This meaneth the vessel of His Spirit, which He shall glorify. Further, what says He? "And there was a river flowing on the right, and from it arose beautiful trees; and whosoever shall eat of them shall live for ever." This meaneth, that we indeed descend into the water full of sins and defilement, but come up, bearing fruit in our heart, having the fear [of God] and trust in Jesus in our spirit. "And whosoever shall eat of these shall live for ever," This meaneth: Whosoever, He declares, shall hear thee speaking, and believe, shall live for ever.

12

THE CROSS OF CHRIST FREQUENTLY ANNOUNCED IN THE OLD TESTAMENT.

In like manner He points to the cross of Christ in another prophet, who saith, "And when shall these things be accomplished? And the Lord saith, When a tree shall be bent down, and again arise, and when blood shall flow out of wood." Here again you have an intimation concerning the cross, and Him who should be crucified. Yet again He speaks of this in Moses, when Israel was attacked by strangers. And that He might remind them, when assailed, that it was on account of their sins they were delivered to death, the Spirit speaks to the heart of Moses, that he should make a figure of the cross, and of Him about to suffer thereon; for unless they put their trust in Him, they shall be overcome for ever. Moses therefore placed one weapon above another in the midst of the hill, and standing upon it, so as to be higher than all the people, he stretched forth his hands, and thus again Israel acquired the mastery. But when again he let down his hands, they were again destroyed. For what reason? That they might know that they could not be saved unless they put their trust in Him. And in another prophet He declares, "All day long I have stretched forth My hands to an unbelieving people, and one that gainsays My righteous way." And again Moses makes a type of Jesus, [signifying] that it was necessary for Him to suffer, [and also] that He would be the author of life [to others], whom they believed to have destroyed on the cross when Israel was failing. For since transgression was committed by Eve through means of the serpent, [the Lord] brought it to pass that every [kind of] serpents bit them, and they died, that He might convince them, that on account of their transgression they were given over to the straits of death. Moreover Moses, when he commanded, "Ye shall not have any graven or molten [image] for your God," did so that he might reveal a type of Jesus. Moses then makes a brazen serpent, and places it upon a beam, and by proclamation assembles the people. When, therefore, they were come together, they besought Moses that he would offer sacrifice in their behalf, and pray for their recovery. And Moses spake unto them, saying, "When any one of you is bitten, let him come to the serpent placed on the pole; and let him hope and believe, that even though dead, it is able to give him life, and immediately he shall be restored." And they did so. Thou hast in this also [an indication of] the glory of Jesus; for in Him and to Him are all things. What, again, says Moses to Jesus (Joshua) the son of Nave, when he gave him this name, as being a prophet, with this view only, that all the people might hear that the Father would reveal all things concerning His Son Jesus to the son of Nave? This name then being given him when he sent him to spy out the land, he said, "Take a book into thy hands, and write what the Lord declares, that the Son of God will in the last days cut off from the roots all the house of Amalek." Behold again: Jesus who was manifested, both by type and in the flesh, is not the Son of man, but the Son of God. Since, therefore, they were to say that Christ was the son of David, fearing and understanding the error of the wicked, he saith, "The Lord said unto my Lord, Sit at My right hand, until I make Thine enemies Thy footstool." And again, thus saith Isaiah, "The Lord said to Christ, my Lord, whose right hand I have holden, that the nations should yield obedience before Him; and I will break in pieces the strength of kings." Behold how David calleth Him Lord and the Son of God.

13

CHRISTIANS, AND NOT JEWS, THE HEIRS OF THE COVENANT.

But let us see if this people is the heir, or the former, and if the covenant belongs to us or to them. Hear ye now what the Scripture saith concerning the people. Isaac prayed for Rebecca his wife, because she was barren; and she conceived. Furthermore also, Rebecca went forth to inquire of the Lord; and the Lord said to her, "Two nations are in thy womb, and two peoples in thy belly; and the one people shall surpass the other, and the eider shall serve the younger." You ought to understand who was Isaac, who Rebecca, and concerning what persons He declared that this people should be greater than that. And in another prophecy Jacob speaks more clearly to his son Joseph, saying, "Behold, the Lord hath not deprived me of thy presence; bring thy sons to me, that I may bless them." And he brought Manasseh and Ephraim, desiring that Manasseh should be blessed, because he was the eider. With this view Joseph led him to the right hand of his father Jacob. But Jacob saw in spirit the type of the people to arise afterwards. And what says [the Scripture]? And Jacob changed the direction of his bands, and laid his fight hand upon the head of Ephraim, the second and younger, and blessed him. And Joseph said to Jacob, "Transfer thy right hand to the head of Manasseh, for he is my first-born son." And Jacob said, "I know it, my son, I know it; but the eider shall serve the younger: yet he also shall be blessed." Ye see on whom he laid [his hands], that this people should be first, and heir of the covenant. If then, still further, the same thing was intimated through Abraham, we reach the perfection of our knowledge. What, then, says He to Abraham? "Because thou hast believed, it is imputed to thee for righteousness: behold, I have made thee the father of those nations who believe in the Lord while in [a state of] uncircumcision."

14

THE LORD HATH GIVEN US THE TESTAMENT WHICH MOSES RECEIVED AND BROKE.

Yes [it is even so]; but let us inquire if the Lord has really given that testament which He swore to the fathers that He would give to the people. He did give it; but they were not worthy to receive it, on account of their sins. For the prophet declares, "And Moses was fasting forty days and forty nights on Mount Sinai, that he might receive the testament of the Lord for the people." And he received from the Lord two tables, written in the spirit by the finger of the hand of the Lord. And Moses having received them, carried them down to give to the people. And the Lord said to Moses, "Moses, Moses, go down quickly; for thy people hath sinned, whom thou didst bring out of the land of Egypt." And Moses understood that they had again made molten images; and he threw the tables out of his hands, and the tables of the testament of the Lord were broken. Moses then received it, but they proved themselves unworthy. Learn now how we have received it. Moses, as a servant, received it; but the Lord himself, having suffered in our behalf, hath given it to us, that we should be the people of inheritance. But He was manifested, in order that they might be perfected in their iniquities, and that we, being constituted heirs through Him, might receive the testament of the Lord Jesus, who was prepared for this end, that by His personal manifestation, redeeming our hearts (which were already wasted by death, and given over to the iniquity of error) from darkness, He might by His word enter into a covenant with us. For it is written how the Father, about to redeem us from darkness, commanded Him to prepare a holy people for Himself. The prophet therefore declares, "I, the Lord Thy God, have called Thee in righteousness, and will hold Thy hand, and will strengthen Thee; and I have given Thee for a covenant to the people, for a light to the nations, to open the eyes of the blind, and to bring forth from fetters them that are bound, and those that sit in darkness out of the prison-house." Ye perceive, then, whence we have been redeemed. And again, the prophet says, "Behold, I have appointed Thee as a light to the nations, that Thou mightest be for salvation even to the ends of the earth, saith the Lord God that redeemeth thee." And again, the prophet saith, "The Spirit of the Lord is upon me; because He hath anointed me to preach the Gospel to the humble: He hath sent me to heal the broken-hearted, to proclaim deliverance to the captives, and recovery of sight to the blind; to announce the acceptable year of the Lord, and the day of recompense; to comfort all that mourn."

15

THE FALSE AND THE TRUE SABBATH.

Further, also, it is written concerning the Sabbath in the Decalogue which [the Lord] spoke, face to face, to Moses on Mount Sinai, "And sanctify ye the Sabbath of the Lord with clean hands and a pure heart." And He says in another place, "If my sons keep the Sabbath, then will I cause my mercy to rest upon them." The Sabbath is mentioned at the beginning of the creation [thus]: "And God made in six days the works of His hands, and made an end on the seventh day, and rested on it, and sanctified it." Attend, my children, to the meaning of this expression, "He finished in six days." This implieth that the Lord will finish all things in six thousand years, for a day is with Him a thousand years. And He Himself testifieth, saying, "Behold, to-day will be as a thousand years." Therefore, my children, in six days, that is, in six thousand years, all things will be finished. "And He rested on the seventh day." This meaneth: when His Son, coming [again], shall destroy the time of the wicked man, and judge the ungodly, and change the-sun, and the moon, and the stars, then shall He truly rest on the seventh day. Moreover, He says, "Thou shalt sanctify it with pure hands and a pure heart." If, therefore, any one can now sanctify the day which God hath sanctified, except he is pure in heart in all things, we are deceived. Behold, therefore: certainly then one properly resting sanctifies it, when we ourselves, having received the promise, wickedness no longer existing, and all things having been made new by the Lord, shall be able to work righteousness. Then we shall be able to sanctify it, having been first sanctified ourselves. Further, He says to them, "Your new moons and your Sabbath I cannot endure." Ye perceive how He speaks: Your present Sabbaths are not acceptable to Me, but that is which I have made, [namely this,] when, giving rest to all things, I shall make a beginning of the eighth day, that is, a beginning of another world. Wherefore, also, we keep the eighth day with joyfulness, the day also on which Jesus rose again from the dead. And when He had manifested Himself, He ascended into the heavens.

16

THE SPIRITUAL TEMPLE OF GOD.

Moreover, I will also tell you concerning the temple, how the wretched [Jews], wandering in error, trusted not in God Himself, but in the temple, as being the house of God. For almost after the manner of the Gentiles they worshipped Him in the temple. But learn how the Lord speaks, when abolishing it: "Who hath meted out heaven with a span, and the earth with his palm? Have not I?""Thus saith the Lord, Heaven is My throne, and the earth My footstool: what kind of house will ye build to Me, or what is the place of My rest?" Ye perceive that their hope is vain. Moreover, He again says, "Behold, they who have cast down this temple, even they shall build it up again." It has so happened. For through their going to war, it was destroyed by their enemies; and now: they, as the servants of their enemies, shall rebuild it. Again, it was revealed that the city and the temple and the people of Israel were to be given up. For the Scripture saith, "And it shall come to pass in the last days, that the Lord will deliver up the sheep of His pasture, and their sheep-fold and tower, to destruction." And it so happened as the Lord had spoken. Let us inquire, then, if there still is a temple of God. There is--where He himself declared He would make and finish it. For it is written, "And it shall come to pass, when the week is completed, the temple of God shall be built in glory in the name of the Lord." I find, therefore, that a temple does exist. Learn, then, how it shall be built in the name of the Lord. Before we believed in God, the habitation of our heart was corrupt and weak, as being indeed like a temple made with hands. For it was full of idolatry, and was a habitation of demons, through our doing such things as were opposed to [the will of] God. But it shall be built, observe ye, in the name of the Lord, in order that the temple of the Lord may be built in glory. How? Learn [as follows]. Having received the forgiveness of sins, and placed our trust in the name of the Lord, we have become new creatures, formed again from the beginning. Wherefore in our habitation God truly dwells in us. How? His word of faith; His calling of promise; the wisdom of the statutes; the commands of the doctrine; He himself prophesying in us; He himself dwelling in us; opening to us who were enslaved by death the doors of the temple, that is, the mouth; and by giving us repentance introduced us into the incorruptible temple. He then, who wishes to be saved, looks not to man, but to Him who dwelleth in him, and speaketh in him, amazed at never having either heard him utter such words with his mouth, nor himself having ever desired to hear them. This is the spiritual temple built for the Lord.

17

CONCLUSION OF THE FIRST PART OF THE EPISTLE.

As far as was possible, and could be done with perspicuity, I cherish the hope that, according to my desire, I have omitted none of those things at present [demanding consideration], which bear upon your salvation. For if I should write to you about things future, ye would not understand, because such knowledge is hid in parables. These things then are so.

18

SECOND PART OF THE EPISTLE. THE TWO WAYS.

But let us now pass to another sort of knowledge and doctrine. There are two ways of doctrine and authority, the one of light, and the other of darkness. But there is a great difference between these two ways. For over one are stationed the light-bringing angels of God, but over the other the angels' of Satan. And He indeed (i.e., God) is Lord for ever and ever, but he (i.e., Satan) is prince of the time of iniquity.

19

THE WAY OF LIGHT.

The way of light, then, is as follows. If any one desires to travel to the appointed place, he must be zealous in his works. The knowledge, therefore, which is given to us for the purpose of walking in this way, is the following. Thou shalt love Him that created thee: thou shalt glorify Him that redeemed thee from death. Thou shalt be simple in heart, and rich in spirit. Thou shalt not join thyself to those who walk in the way of death. Thou shalt hate doing what is unpleasing to God: thou shalt hate all hypocrisy. Thou shalt not forsake the commandments of the Lord. Thou shalt not exalt thyself, but shalt be of a lowly mind. Thou shalt not take glory to thyself. Thou shalt not take evil counsel against thy neighbour. Thou shalt not allow over-boldness to enter into thy soul. Thou shalt not commit fornication: thou shalt not commit adultery: thou shalt not be a corrupter of youth. Thou shalt not let the word of God issue from thy lips with any kind of impurity. Thou shalt not accept persons when thou reprovest any one for transgression. Thou shalt be meek: thou shalt be peaceable. Thou shalt tremble at the words which thou hearest. Thou shalt not be mindful of evil against thy brother. Thou shalt not be of doubtful mind as to whether a thing shall be or not. Thou shalt not take the name of the Lord in vain. Thou shalt love thy neighbour more than thine own soul. Thou shalt not slay the child by procuring abortion; nor, again, shalt thou destroy it after it is born. Thou shalt not withdraw thy hand from thy son, or from thy daughter, but from their infancy thou shalt teach them the fear of the Lord. Thou shalt not covet what is thy neighbour's, nor shalt thou be avaricious. Thou shalt not be joined in soul with the haughty, but thou shalt be reckoned With the righteous and lowly. Receive thou as good things the trials which come upon thee. Thou shalt not be of double mind or of double tongue, for a double tongue is a snare of death. Thou shalt be subject to the Lord, and to [other] masters as the image of God, with modesty and fear. Thou shalt not issue orders with bitterness to thy maidservant or thy man-servant, who trust in the same [God], lest thou shouldst not reverence that God who is above both; for He came to call men not according to their outward appearance, but according as the Spirit had prepared them. Thou shalt communicate in all things with thy neighbour; thou shalt not call things thine own; for if ye are partakers in common of things which are incorruptible, how much more [should you be] of those things which are corruptible! Thou shalt not be hasty with thy tongue, for the mouth is a snare of death. As far as possible, thou shalt be pure in thy soul. Do not be ready to stretch forth thy hands to take, whilst thou contractest them to give. Thou shalt love, as the apple of thine eye, every one that speaketh to thee the word of the Lord. Thou shalt remember the day of judgment, night and day. Thou shalt seek out every day the faces of the saints, either by word examining them, and going to exhort them, and meditating how to save a soul by the word, or by thy hands thou shalt labour for the redemption of thy sins. Thou shalt not hesitate to give, nor murmur when thou givest. "Give to every one that asketh thee," and thou shalt know who is the good Recompenser of the reward. Thou shalt preserve what thou hast received [in charge], neither adding to it nor taking from it. To the last thou shalt hate the wicked [one]. Thou shalt judge righteously. Thou shalt not make a schism, but thou shalt pacify those that contend by bringing them together. Thou shalt confess thy sins. Thou shalt not go to prayer with an evil conscience. This is the way of light.

20

THE WAY OF DARKNESS.

But the way of darkness is crooked, and full of cursing; for it is the way of eternal death with punishment, in which way are the things that destroy the soul, viz., idolatry, over-confidence, the arrogance of power, hypocrisy, double-heartedness, adultery, murder, rapine, haughtiness, transgression, deceit, malice, self-sufficiency, poisoning, magic, avarice, want of the fear of God. [In this way, too,] are those who persecute the good, those who hate truth, those who love falsehood, those who know not the reward of righteousness, those who cleave not to that which is good, those who attend not with just judgment to the widow and orphan, those who watch not to the fear of God, [but incline] to wickedness, from whom meekness and patience are far off; persons who love vanity, follow after a reward, pity not the needy, labour not in aid of him who is overcome with toil; who are prone to evil-speaking, who know not Him that made them, who are murderers of children, destroyers of the workmanship of God; who turn away him that is in want, who oppress the afflicted, who are advocates of the rich, who are unjust judges of the poor, and who are in every respect transgressors.

21

CONCLUSION.

It is well, therefore, that he who has learned the judgments of the Lord, as many as have been written, should walk in them. For he who keepeth these shall be glorified in the kingdom of God; but he who chooseth other things shall be destroyed with his works. On this account there will be a resurrection, on this account a retribution. I beseech you who are superiors, if you will receive any counsel of my good-will, have among yourselves those to whom you may show kindness: do not forsake them. For the day is at hand on which all things shall perish with the evil [one]. The Lord is near, and His reward. Again, and yet again, I beseech you: be good lawgivers to one another; continue faithful counsellors of one another; take away from among you all hypocrisy. And may God, who ruleth over all the world, give to you wisdom, intelligence, understanding, knowledge of His judgments, with patience. And be ye taught of God, inquiring diligently what the Lord asks from you; and do it that ye may be safe in the day of judgment. And if you have any remembrance of what is good, be mindful of me, meditating on these things, in order that both my desire and watchfulness may result in some good. I beseech you, entreating this as a favour. While yet you are in this fair vessel, do not fail in any one of those things, but unceasingly seek after them, and fulfil every commandment; for these things are worthy. Wherefore I have been the more earnest to write to you, as my ability served, that I might cheer you. Farewell, ye children of love and peace. The Lord of glory and of all grace be with your spirit. Amen.

Copyright © 2020 by FV Editions
Cover Design : FVE
Ebook ISBN : 979-10-299-0883-5
Paperback ISBN : 9798639253317
Hardcover ISBN : 979-10-299-0884-2
All rights reserved.

www.ingramcontent.com/pod-product-compliance
Lightning Source LLC
LaVergne TN
LVHW042247070526
838201LV00089B/65